Anthony Bourdain: *

Chef Anthony Bourdain, more famous for his personality and philosophy than his culinary creations, followed a unique trajectory in his career and paved the way for a new type of writing, presentation, and discussion of food and culture. Bourdain saw society through the prism of food, and at one point, late in his career, even told an interviewer that food was essentially 'boring.' What was interesting, Bourdain claimed, was the context. Who was at the table, what music was playing, "was there a dog." Bourdain worked over half of his life, literally and figuratively, underground; he spent his time in restaurant kitchens, either recovering from drugs, in the throes of chemical bliss, or pits of depression. Bourdain worked intense shifts, churning out at times French classics and at other times food he loved to mock and ridicule later, most notably Eggs Benedict. In 2000, the success of Bourdain's book *Kitchen Confidential* resulted in a shift from an insular existence, making food for others, to that of a statesman and world-traveler, knee-deep in a food revolution, consuming and commenting on food that others made for him. Bourdain bridged several careers and, in doing so, created a new one. Bourdain, who died at 61 of suicide, celebrated life and gave moral and spiritual virtuosity to what could have been thought of as simple hedonism. In his later life, Bourdain began to walk the tightrope between anthropology and journalism, calling attention to humanitarian disasters in Gaza, crises in Lebanon, and diving headfirst into the catastrophic repercussions of United States global policy in places like Cambodia and Laos. Bourdain jokingly referred to this career as not-working and boasted about having the best job in the world. Self-deprecating at times and arrogant and audacious at others, Bourdain's TV shows and books reached millions of readers and viewers, and the tragedy of his death resulted in a global outpouring of grief and regret. The life that Bourdain lived, however, continues to endure in the hearts, minds, and imaginations of his fans, his friends, and his family.

Anthony Bourdain was born on June 25, 1956, to Gladys and Pierre Bourdain while America was beginning its second year in the Vietnam War. Bourdain described himself as a kid from the Jersey suburbs, attempting to convey the uneventfulness of his childhood home, but as a child he had his eye set on distant shores and worshipped alternative lifestyles. At twelve years old, Bourdain was already a huge fan of Hunter S. Thompson, and as an adolescent read George Orwell, William Burroughs, Lester Bangs, and was listening to the Stooges, the Dolls, Roxy Music, the Velvets and the Ramones. Bourdain's parents divorced, but Bourdain never disclosed much about how this event impacted his life. Gladys worked as a staff editor for the *New York Times* and Pierre was an executive in the classical music industry. Bourdain spoke fondly of his father in his last major book, *Medium Raw*, reminiscing about times his father would hold him on his shoulders and striding into the plunging waves of the Jersey Shore, and in an article for *Bon Appetit*, he wrote that his father was the one who first impressed upon him the vital importance of respecting those you eat with and those who prepare food for you. For the rest of Bourdain's life, he emphasized the supreme importance of being a respectful guest and recognizing the generosity of spirit that cooking for a stranger or guest implies. Bourdain famously consumed an uncooked warthog anus in Namibia out of respect for his hosts, so it is clear he took his father's advice to heart. Pierre Bourdain died in 1987 at the age of fifty-eight of a heart attack, but his guidance stayed with Anthony past death. As a child, Anthony went on a family trip to France, which was the first time he remembered leaving the country. Tasting vichyssoise soup was revolutionary and introduced the idea to Bourdain that food could be a source of pleasure, like music or literature. His true revelation came, however, when he ate an oyster that a neighbor picked out straight from the ocean and the unexpected salty, silky brine filled his mouth and lifted his spirit. Bourdain continued to refer to this moment as an important turning point, one that set him on a quest to find new and great experiences of sensory bliss from the world around him for the rest of his life; he even went so far as describing the moment as Proustian. Bourdain said in an interview, "The food, the long and often stupid and self-destructive search for the next thing, whether it was sex or drugs or some other new sensation, would all stem from this moment." Sensory bliss was not an uncommon goal as a teenager growing up in the seventies, where cocaine was practically touted as a natural and risk-free source of happiness and AIDS was still a few years away. Bourdain followed his girlfriend, Nancy Putkoski, to college at Vassar College in Dutchess County in New York, and began to experiment with and abuse drugs, beginning with marijuana and cocaine and ending with heroin, buying his first bag on Rivington Street in 1980 at 24 years old. Bourdain describes his college as a place where women were the majority and the environment of Provincetown as open and libertine, but he still was kicked out or quit school after a mishap involving "a depraved incident and a firearm." Bourdain lingered, however, finding employment at a clam and flounder shack in Provincetown. This first experience in the kitchen proved formative. Bourdain, discussing his experience on the Letterman Show in 2001, described looking over at the kitchen staff and noting that they dressed like pirates, did drugs, drank free liquor, ate free food and were romantically very active. "It looked pretty good to me," he said with a sheepish grin. Bourdain described his culinary beginnings similarly on a range of occasions, perhaps most poignantly discussing what draws people to the kitchen in an interview with the blog First We Feast before his 60th birthday.

"If there's a constant in the chef story it's the story of lost boys. That's the chef story I keep coming back to again and again, the chef story of actively abused or neglected children. Marco Pierre White. Gordon Ramsay. Eric Ripert. Very different backgrounds, but there's a lonely boy in so many of these story arcs somewhere. That's a regular feature in chefs... I think it's something that people on TV, people who write, people who cook share: this difficulty in giving love and receiving love. They just don't quite know how to do it. Not comfortable with what seems normal for everybody else."

The image Bourdain paints of the kitchen staff verges from motley pirate crew to the mob, where there are strong superstructures, but each man determines his or her own fate. Bourdain describes the restaurant scene as the first time he felt comfortable within a structure and proud of the work he could do within that structure. Throughout his career Bourdain referred to his kitchen work as the real challenge of his life and much of his language. Physical work requiring stamina, patience and diligence were strengths Bourdain continued to value for the rest of his life. In an interview for *Men's Journal*, Bourdain states, "I'm a very busy guy. I would say that I work hard ... And then to go to Southeast Asia ... you're constantly confronted with what work really can mean. I love rice country for that reason. Any place where people grow rice. You see people bent at the hip, re-planting rice, eight, 10 hours a day. It puts words like 'work' into perspective." Bourdain was able to identify with laborers around the world and in a sense, his work in the kitchen humbled him and prepared him for the career which was to come. Bourdain's personality also grew during these years. Bourdain's vernacular comes from his time putting in grueling hours with the lowest kitchen staff on the totem pole, completely removed from those on the other side. Bourdain also liked to describe as an observation that if any chef could play a guitar or a bass, there would be no fine dining because the attraction was the same. Restaurant workers wanted to live without consequences, have fun and be free, much like those in the music industry. Bourdain worked his way up from dishwasher and began to think more seriously about food and cooking. In 1975, Bourdain attended the Culinary Institute of America in New Hyde Park, graduated in 1978, and soon afterwards moved to

New York with Putkoski into an apartment on Riverside Drive. Anthony and Nancy were married in 1985.

The glamour Bourdain attributed to the life of a restaurant worker also applied to the life of drugs and alcohol. Marijuana and cocaine were regular companions during long shifts and in life outside of work, and those soon gave way to heroin. What followed were seven years of living for nearly nothing else. Bourdain riffed in an interview for *Men's Journal*, "If heroin is your number one thing on your list of things to do for the day, there is no number two." Bourdain likened his relationship with Putkoski as one similar to that of the couple in the Gus San Vant film *Drugstore Cowboy,* where a couple commits crimes to fund their drug habit. Bourdain recalls a sense of pride at his first withdrawal, and heroin fit in perfectly to the romantic vision of bohemian warrior, akin to Hunter S. Thompson or many of the musicians of the day. Bourdain glamorized the life of the criminal, and much of his writing of the time positions himself as such, in vaguely masked forms. Always a lanky chef on the edge of capture, adrenaline-fueled and scandalous.

Bourdain's ambitions as a writer date back to his early years. Bourdain reportedly wrote term papers for his fellow students at Vassar in exchange for drugs, and had always had a facile dexterity with language, writing in a colloquial vernacular which he said came naturally and pleased him. Bourdain really began to thrive when he took a writing class given by the esteemed editor and writer, Gordon Lish. Gordon Lish, when asked later, did not recall Bourdain, but the impact of the class on Bourdain was said to be so profound to make Bourdain refer to life "before and after Lish." Bourdain's life throughout his twenties remained saturated with drug use, and it was not until 1987, two years after he took the writing class, that he was able to kick heroin altogether, with the help of methadone. Here Bourdain also connected his idea of internal motivation with inner self-concept, claiming that it was only when he began to look in the mirror and not like what he saw that he started to want to change. In his article for *Men's Journal* in 2014, he addresses this change by stating

> "My vanity would not allow it. Also, vanity saved me from heroin, a lot of people, with what they call, 'low self-esteem', if you look at anyone getting rogered on a dirty couch by Ron Jeremy in the history of film, chances are you're going to find a self-esteem problem. That's true with people who have the most trouble getting off hard drugs. When they look in the mirror, they don't see someone worth saving. I looked in the mirror, and I was very unhappy, and embarrassed by the guy I saw there. And I think that's what provided me with the will to kick narcotics,

because I was too fucking vain to be that guy anymore. That whining, desperate, sick, fucking victim."

Bourdain did not go completely sober, however, replacing heroin with cocaine, and recalls low moments scraping chips of crack cocaine from shag carpets to smoke immediately, and having to sell his records on the street to make a few dollars one Christmas after his recovery. Despite these setbacks, Bourdain was busy, working intense hours in closet-like spaces. Bourdain worked at the buffet table at the Rainbow Room, was a sous-chef at W.P.A., Chuck Howard's, Nikki and Kelly, Gianni's, the Supper Club and many other in-between establishments while he was in different phases of addiction and recovery. Bourdain's life, working, hustling to make money to afford drugs, doing drugs, being in love with Nancy, and never fully putting down a pen and paper provide the fodder for *Kitchen Confidential* and provided Bourdain with what he later described as an incredible 'bullshit meter.' That said, Bourdain was always mystified when anyone walked away from his tales of this time with anything but cautionary horror. Finally, in 1998 Bourdain landed a job as executive chef at Les Halles. Here Bourdain could take pride in his craft and was no longer the lowest but the highest on the kitchen totem pole. Bourdain was a traditionalist and day after day churned out sterling classics like Steak Béarnaise and Coq Au Vin.

Fame was to come to Bourdain, however, not through any result of his sweat and tears in the kitchen, but rather through the world's sudden desire for his personal voice through his writing. Bourdain had written two crime novels starting in 1995, *A Bone in the Throat* and *Gone Bamboo,* whose reception fell flat and production was soon discontinued. Still, Bourdain financed his own book tour, and talked later about watching people awkwardly file past his little table, stacks of books unperturbed, attempting desperately not to make eye contact. The protagonists of these novels bear striking resemblance to Bourdain's own self, chefs at French restaurants who are long, lanky, and even in one case have Bourdain's one pierced ear. Later Bourdain referred to these works as types of therapy, and ironically referred to his relief at writing about something other than himself, despite the works' clear autobiographical underpinnings. Bourdain sent manuscripts to his writer friend, Joel Rose, with no response, and it wasn't before April 19, 1999, when the *New Yorker* chose to publish his article "Don't Read Before Eating" that Bourdain's big break came. Bourdain wouldn't have had the chutzpah to even send his article in if the *New York Press*, which originally intended to publish the piece, stalled publication for months and his mother suggested submission to the *New Yorker*, saying she knew someone who worked there and could make sure they read his piece.

Bourdain took a chance and the *New Yorker* accepted his essay. What followed for Bourdain was like night and day. The article attempted to shatter the pristine facade of the culture of eating out at nice restaurants in New York. Bread that was in your basket had most likely been on the basket of the past two tables before you, and the floor of a restaurant was thought of nearly as a giant napkin. Meat cooked well done was most likely to be the gristliest piece of animal available and fish served on Monday was most likely caught on Wednesday. Hollandaise sauce offered perfect copulation ground for bacteria, and the real premise for brunch as a cultural event was to get rid of whatever couldn't get sold over the weekend. Bourdain paints the life of the chef as a glamorous, lawless, hard-scrabble gangster, whose constant hustle produces the same camaraderie and loyal bonds as ex-convicts, without requiring time in jail. Bourdain was always a fan of the cult classic *The Warriors*, and his understanding and depiction of kitchen life was not far off from this model for relationships. Bourdain, who thought that only chefs would have an interest in reading his piece, captured the imagination of thousands, and the next day there was a press team outside of Les Halles, where Bourdain was still working. People were fascinated and, in glamorizing the life of the chef, Bourdain himself became an object of interest. Journalists were waiting for him at work the next day and Bourdain quickly saw his life change dramatically. Almost immediately after the article was published, Bourdain signed a book deal with Karen Rinaldi, the wife of NPR journalist Joel Rose, for $50,000. Deeply in debt with unpaid credit card bills, in trouble with the IRS, without health insurance or an escape plan, Bourdain leapt at this deal and took the opportunity seriously, producing the book *Kitchen Confidential* in 2000. Bourdain has related his focus and drive in producing this book with his many failed attempts in his previous lives. He has said of chefs in general that they are self-sabotaging, using the metaphor of someone constantly trying to fix a lightbulb while simultaneously kicking the stool out from under their feet. For *Kitchen Confidential*, however, Bourdain gave his all, and the book was met with spectacular success and accolades. Bourdain modeled his book in part after George Orwell's *Down and Out in Paris and London* and the image of a chef in part off of Marco Pierre White in *White Heat*. The book that Bourdain was skeptical would garner interest outside of the small circle of restaurant chefs has now sold millions of copies and is cited frequently as a revolutionary tome of food writing.

After *Kitchen Confidential*, Bourdain continued to work at Les Halles, not realizing that his life was about to change dramatically. Bourdain speaks of wanting to keep his day job to be able to pay the bills, and when the Food

Network approached Bourdain with talks of a television show, Bourdain, who had never worked in TV, also said yes. There were conditions, however, as Bourdain was instinctively careful to maintain his image. Bourdain had seen TV Chefs like Emeril Lagasse as exemplifying his antithesis, with shiny, contained, and clean visions of kitchen life. Bourdain wanted none of that.

As a follow-up to *Kitchen Confidential*, Bourdain had been considering a book in which he travelled around the world, trying new food and writing about his adventures. Bourdain had the opportunity to help open the Tokyo version of Les Halles and had come back blown away. Since his trip to France as a kid and the occasional trips to the Caribbean with Putkoski, Bourdain had not travelled much, and spent most of his days with the same group of people in a series of hot, small, windowless rooms that were New York City kitchens. The Food Network agreed to fund this endeavor, and film it, and "A Cook's Tour" was born. As new doors opened for Bourdain, he chose to close the window through which he had snuck out. Putkoski, who had been his companion for nearly 30 years, would not accompany Bourdain for this next part of his journey. Unwilling to be constantly travelling and unenthused with the new fame that had transformed their lives nearly overnight, Putkoski and Bourdain divorced after a few episodes, ending the longest relationship of Bourdain's life. Putkoski confided to a journalist that she was surprised when it ended. She had thought shared experiences "bulletproofed" their relationship and that nothing could tear them apart. The last time she would hear from Bourdain would be after he went through a moment of personal crisis in the late 2000s. Reacting to a bad side effect of a medication, alone in the oyster village where he had first fell in love with food, Bourdain wrote a letter to Putkoski, apologizing for their separation. According to Putkoski, Bourdain wrote, "'I'm fucking sorry. I'm sure I've acted like I wasn't.' We've had very little contact—you know, civil, but very, very little. 'I'm sorry. I know that doesn't help. It won't fix it, there's no making amends. But it's not like I don't remember. It's not like I don't know what I've done.'" The television show, meanwhile, met with great success, and thus began the setup for a series of shows which would culminate in *Anthony Bourdain: Parts Unknown*, and position Bourdain as the American statesman and most visible food anthropologist of our time.

A Cook's Tour allowed Bourdain to see the world and it became clear what type of exploration Bourdain was interested in right away. The recipe for cooking shows was stale and in Bourdain's vision, useless. The idea of filming scene after scene of souffles, tartlets, and stews entering a host's mouth, with loud visceral reactions and long interviews with other chefs bored Bourdain, and he attempted to turn the camera outward and illuminate the people and cultures he was visiting. Bourdain frequently positioned his work with food as a vehicle to culture. Bourdain once marveled in an interview that all he had to do was ask a simple question relating to food and soon the conversation had grown a thousand different legs, and someone from a new world was opening up to him about a new experience, and frequently one to which he could relate. Bourdain's persona helped him relate to people from all walks of life, and his candidness about his drug use gave him the unique position of being able to look down his nose at no man but also sharply criticize those who looked down their noses at others. Bourdain's show was also contradictory, as it was in some sense about the entire world and in some sense entirely about Bourdain. The opening monologue for the first episode of *A Cook's Tour* is revealing. "As a cook, tastes and smells are my memories, now I'm in search of some new ones. So I'm leaving New York City and hope to have a few epiphanies around the world and I'm willing to go to some length to do that. I'm looking for extremes of emotion and experience. I'll try anything, I'll risk everything, I have nothing to lose." With these few words, Bourdain positioned his show around the idea that through travel and exposure to a variety of cultures we can have independent revelations that will teach us or enlighten us about how to live.

A Cook's Tour began in Tokyo, where Bourdain had last travelled when opening Les Halles. Bourdain visits the fish market and learns about the diet of Sumo Wrestlers. In a sense, we are seeing Bourdain see the world and begin to see himself. After this episode, there comes Vietnam, Cambodia, Portugal, Spain, France, Morocco, Russia, Mexico, England, St. Martin and Brazil, Australia, Singapore, Thailand and a smattering of places in the United States. Bourdain's excitement and energy are palpable as he begins this exploration which would last the rest of his life, and in 2001 he published a book by the same name, *A Cook's Tour*, reflecting on what he experienced during the filming of the show. Bourdain had also mysteriously written a historical biography of Typhoid Mary and another mystery featuring another 'lovable criminal' called the *Bobby Gold Stories*, which fell mostly under the radar, although this new book was reviewed in the *New York Times* with moderate praise, underlying Bourdain's strengths in painting a picture of the emotional rather than gustatory aspects of food that can be missing in food writing. Bourdain published another version of *A Cook's Tour* the following year in 2002, and in 2004 he published a cookbook of Les Halles recipes, as he was still, at least in name, the executive chef. Most of Bourdain's literary work after *Kitchen Confidential* was met with mixed reviews, and no book of his sold more than the first book, but the astounding success of Bourdain's TV shows created what will most likely be his most lasting legacy. Bourdain also used his fame to serve as a mentor to several important chefs, willing to step in to help a career that was in trouble, and also to make connections which in many instances would turn into long-lasting friendships.

After *A Cook's Tour*, Bourdain shifted what was essentially the same show over to the Travel Channel and renamed it *No Reservations*. Even the new title reached toward the shifting emphasis of the show. No longer was Anthony thought of as a chef on tour of the world, but rather a consumer of food, looking to see through the cracks into the heart of the world through food, culture, and conversation. Bourdain also continued to write, publishing *The Nasty Bits* in 2006, which was once again met with limited praise and smaller sales. *No Reservations*, however, was immensely popular. The show ran for nine seasons, taking Bourdain and his crew to France, Iceland, back to Southeast Asia in Vietnam and Malaysia, Uzbekistan, New Zealand, China, Japan, Peru, Quebec, Sweden, Puerto Rico, India, Korea, Ghana, Namibia and more. When Anthony Bourdain died, he had visited almost one hundred countries, eaten at countless amazing restaurants, and become close friends with a large variety of the best chefs in the world. The first episode of *No Reservations* began in France in 2005 and the last episode ended in Brooklyn in 2012.

During this time, Bourdain also got married again and had a child, something that seemed light years away during the darker years of his twenties. One of Bourdain's greatest joys was the friendship he cultivated with chef Eric Ripert, head chef and owner of Le Bernardin Restaurant in New York. Ripert, a starring guest on many of Bourdain's shows, decided to set up Bourdain with Ottavia Busia, a hostess at his restaurant. Ottavia had moved to New York with $300 in her bank account, pursuing a love with an Irish rocker, dropping out of dental school, and was nearly as dedicated to her job as Bourdain was to his. Ripert, knowing Bourdain's difficult schedule, assumed that they could have a pleasant one-night stand and that would be the end of it. The two hit it off, and on their second date got matching chef's knife tattoos. Then something happened that radically changed their course.

On one of the episode of *No Reservations*, Bourdain and his team fly to Beirut expecting to nibble on koffee and enjoy the vibrant nightlife so famous in Lebanon. Instead, war broke out soon after they arrived, and they spent the episode barricaded in a hotel, watching bombs go off on the people below. Bourdain never considered himself a journalist, but later would describe how this event changed his understanding of journalism and his role in the media landscape. Keefe writes in his *New Yorker* profile, "In Hanoi, one of Obama's staffers told him that, until the episode aired, some people in the White House had been unaware of the extent of the unexploded-ordnance problem in Laos. Very casually, he said, 'So I guess you do some good after all,'" Bourdain recalled. "I'm a little embarrassed. I feel like Bono. I don't want to be that guy. The show is always about me. I would be bullshitting you if I said I was on some mission. I'm not." Bourdain insists that this is not the case. "I'm not going to the White House Correspondents' dinner," he said. "I don't need to be laughing it up with Henry Kissinger." He then launched into a tirade about how it sickens him, having travelled in Southeast Asia, to see Kissinger embraced by the power-lunch crowd. "Any journalist who has ever been polite to Henry Kissinger, you know, fuck that person," he said, his indignation rising. "I'm a big believer in moral gray areas, but, when it comes to that guy, in my view he should not be able to eat at a restaurant in New York." Notably, Bourdain said, what he was seeing on TV was so different from what was happening on the ground. Perhaps Bourdain hadn't connected the news bytes about politics with their reality, and much as nothing except washing thousands upon thousands of dishes could teach Bourdain the tangible feel of hard work, nothing but experiencing violence, fear, and chaos could provoke in Bourdain a streak of political activism. What the event provoked, however, in Bourdain's personal life, was a sudden impetus to speed things up with Busia. Busia and Bourdain decided, as it were, to "spin the wheel," marry and have a child. Busia remarked playfully that Bourdain had "old sperm" and the time was now, and she was also nearly 40. Their child Ariane was born in 2007, and Bourdain talked frequently in interviews about how the experience of having a daughter gave him great happiness and helped reframe his relationship with women.

Instead of slowing down, however, Bourdain's career just increased in speed. Bourdain published a book, *Medium Raw*, which again met with mixed reviews. The *New York Times* review was less than positive, or even neutral, "Unfortunately, as the title of his new essay collection, 'Medium Raw,' warns, he gives it to us half-cooked." As Bourdain became more and more familiar with the world through TV production and cinematography, the shows became more and more about the world around Bourdain and less about the food or about his own personal journey. Bourdain also wanted to focus more on the people he was able to interview in various places, and his next show, *The Layover* (also for the Travel Channel), demonstrated this change. *The Layover* ran for two seasons, followed by one season of a show called *The Getaway*, and then a movie adaptation of one of his earlier novels, *Bone in the Throat*, in 2015. Directed by Graham Henman and starring Vanessa Kirby and Ed Westwick, Bourdain was the executive producer and must have found great pleasure in seeing his old protagonists come to life. After the birth of Ariane, Busia took up Jiu Jitsu and convinced Bourdain to do the same. Busia, however, was to eventually dedicate nearly her entire life towards becoming a master at Jiu Jitsu, whereas Bourdain took up the sport more as a hobby. The couple was together for nine years, but around 2015 they began to talk openly about how their marriage was effectively over and they were separated. Both individuals had chosen their own passions over the ability to spend time with the other, Busia focusing on her Jiu Jitsu and Bourdain keeping up a schedule that only allowed him to spend time in New York at most twenty weeks of the year.

At this point in his career, Bourdain was beginning to fully take advantage of the freedom his fame and resources allowed. Bourdain was always a film buff, and this is what inspired him in this new freedom. As a child, he recalls watching important films by Mel Brooks and Stanley Kubrick. In interviews, Bourdain, an exigent boss, stated the necessity of working with individuals with as profound a knowledge of film, as he would find it necessary to be understood when referencing this scene or that cinematographic style. At this stage in his career, then, Bourdain was also able to work with famous directors, inviting guests to direct specific episodes of his shows. Bourdain also befriended directors, travelling to Madagascar with Darren Aronofsky and directing one of his final episodes with Christopher Doyle.

Bourdain was also participating in side projects. Notably, Bourdain, in a twist of fate, published a book with writer and friend, Joel Rose, to whom Bourdain had sent manuscript after manuscript as a young man, hoping for publication. Instead, Bourdain, a huge fan of graphic novelists like Robert Crumb, a graphic novel called *Get Jiro!* In 2012 with Rose and Langdon Foss. This novel centers on Japanese folkloric horror stories, focusing on *yōkai* and *yūrei*, traditional demons and Japanese cuisine. They would follow this novel in 2018 with *Hungry Ghost*, this time a collaboration between Bourdain, Rose, Alberto Ponticelli, and Vanesa del Rey.

In the filming of *Parts Unknown*, Bourdain had also forever changed what it meant to make a TV show about food and culture. There were copycat shows and whole genres of television that appeared, stemming from aspects of Bourdain's repertoire, like the Bizarre Foods trend, but Bourdain was the one creating the industry standard. Eddie Huang, creator of the restaurant Baohaus and comedic TV show *Fresh Off the Boat*, remarked on this truth after

Bourdain's passing. Huang wrote for *the Rolling Stone*, "You don't realize how much someone means to you when you're chasing them like a greyhound. They're your inspiration, your role-model, your North Star. I don't think any of us would be the people we are without Tony setting the standard not just as a writer, not just as a host or spirit guide, but as a human that always made it his duty to pick someone up that was down." Bourdain wanted to shift the focus in food television from the food to the situations that made the food possible, the role of the food in the lives of individuals, and what the food symbolizes or represents about each culture. Bourdain was also deeply curious about people and wanted to connect with others as much as possible, looking for how they answered questions that he asked himself every day.

Bourdain famously met President Obama for an episode of *Parts Unknown* in Hanoi. They met at a modest eatery that served one dish, a pork, noodle, and soup medley called Bún-chả. With the president's meal and beer, the total came out to around six dollars. The next day, when Bourdain scooted through town on his blue vespa, he recalled in an interview the reaction of the hundreds of Hanoi citizens who came up to him in tears, not because the president had come to Hanoi, but because he had eaten the food they themselves would eat. Bourdain pointed out frequently this intersection between politics and food, in the sense that there is a great deal of politics involved in who gets to eat what. When shooting a scene in Egypt before the Revolution, the military attempted to censor their footage of Egyptians eating Ful, which was a type of mushy, soupy beans that was an incredibly pervasive street food. Bourdain later realized that the reason they didn't want the shot aired, which was aired anyway thanks to some sneaky maneuvering on the part of the crew, was because the show aired in Egypt, and the reality was that for many Egyptians, Ful was all there was to eat. The government thought that airing this practice on TV would draw it into too sharp a contrast with the other countries featured and create a rebellion. Bourdain told a Canadian interviewer in 2016 that politics and food were intrinsically linked, saying "there's nothing more political, there's nothing more revealing of whether something works on the ground...it's difficult to spend time in Cuba thinking, wow this seems to work out for people..." Bourdain therefore could not avoid politics in his travels, and instead of glossing over the tragedy that had plagued countries, Bourdain sought to bring it to the surface, without turning away pleasure-seeking viewers. Bourdain, however, never considered himself a journalist because he always saw his prime motivation as manipulative and selfish. At his heart, he reflected, he had a strong belief about something and wanted his viewers to feel the same thing, which he hoped to achieve through the way he framed his interviews and created film.

The most celebrated essay of *Medium Raw* is titled "My Aim Is True," wherein Bourdain describes the life and practice of the fish butcher for Le Bernardin, Justo Thomas. The attention to detail and clear admiration Bourdain feels for Thomas' ability to recreate perfection against enormous odds every evening stands out. "Halibut, white tuna, black sea bass, mahi mahi, red snapper, skate, cod, monkfish, or salmon, mostly unscaled, on the bone, guts still in, reaches halfway up the wall of his tiny workspace." Le Bernardin is arguably the best seafood restaurant in America, with four consecutive four star reviews and a two-time three Michelin star winner. The essay ends with the commentary that in the majority of cases, kitchen staff can never afford to eat at the restaurants for which they toil, including Thomas. Bourdain invites Thomas to dine at Le Bernardin's restaurant, however, and he describes sitting with Thomas, finally seeing the product of his work, discussing inequality, the way of the world, and the life goals of Thomas. In this story, Bourdain shows his elevation of the working man, which sets him apart from other food commentators and critics. Not all the subjects were this positive, however; Bourdain also criticizes Alice Waters in *Medium Raw* for what he saw as tone-deafness surrounding the economic availability of organic food. Bourdain respected good food that was made well and was unpretentious that created good conversation, warm feelings, and lasting bonds. In 2016 Bourdain came out with his own cookbook, *Appetites*, around the time of his ultimate separation and the beginning of a love affair which would be the last of his life with the actress Asia Argento. *Appetites* focused on the way Bourdain cooked for his daughter and represented exactly the type of cooking he championed in his shows. Bourdain reflected in an interview that in some ways he wished he could be the patriarch who lived surrounded by his wife, children, and grandchildren, for the most part staying put. This lifestyle, however, was incompatible with Bourdain's personality, and he reflected in *People* magazine shortly before he died that he never saw himself retiring.

Bourdain had influence in his own work, through his influence on others, and had his hand in a number of different pies, including David Chang's *Mind of a Chef* and, most recently, Christiane Amanpour's series for CNN focusing on sex and relationships around the world. Bourdain also had an imprint at Ecco publishing, through which he intended to amplify the voices of lesser-known, more controversial authors who could not gain prestige elsewhere. One of the more surprising choices of work on behalf of Bourdain's company was the foreword he wrote for the food critic Marilyn Hagerty, whose work had gone viral after a rapturous review of Olive Garden. Bourdain, while at first joining in on the joke, later repented and reflected that this type of writing was part of the larger trend of people of all walks of life taking part in a larger culinary experience, reflecting on eating habits, which was mostly positive. Bourdain also produced a documentary about the influential chef Jeremiah Tower, called *Jeremiah Tower: The Last Magnificent*, and worked on a movie surrounding food waste called *Wasted! The Story of Food Waste*. Many of these new film ventures were the work of his new production company, Zero Point Zero. Bourdain also represented this new desire to showcase the work of others in *Anthony Bourdain Presents: RAD Stories*. In addition to all this work, Bourdain was also deeply involved in a plan to bring a Singapore-style, open-air market to Pier 57, which would be an enormous enterprise. Like Mario Batali's Eataly, Bourdain Market was to show the work of a chef or culinary expert through the selection of vendors and architectural arrangement of the establishment. Bourdain's plan was to travel to Southeast Asia, picking up vendors to bring back with him if willing for business in the market, but the plan ran into problems when obtaining visas were more difficult than expected, licensing became an issue, and profitability questioned, and ultimately Bourdain never signed the lease. (Google ended up renting the space.)

Bourdain was a strange mix of vanity and humanity. Bourdain, in part because of his past experiences with drugs and the long years he put in as a dishwasher and line cook, did not consider himself above anyone by virtue of his skin, sex, or creed. Bourdain was able to visit strange cultures without tokenizing them, a difficult trap for some white male chefs to avoid. Bourdain took people seriously and treated everyone with respect. He was adamant that eating dinner with someone who treated the waitstaff poorly would mean he never ate dinner with them again. Huang describes watching Bourdain's "Asia Special" episode with his family. Writing for *Rolling Stone*, he says "there was something about Tony that screamed, 'I'm not like other white people. I'm not here to laugh at you.' He didn't see dirty immigrants and aliens; he saw fully formed 360-degree humans containing old ways and wisdom manifested in food." Bourdain, a man who in some sense spent a great bulk of his life seeking enlightenment and knowledge, did not believe in judgment (except in certain cases). In his *New Yorker* Profile, Keefe writes, "After Bourdain read 'How to Live,' Sarah Bakewell's 2010 book about Michel de Montaigne, he got a tattoo

on his forearm of Montaigne's motto, in ancient Greek: 'I suspend judgment.'"
In an article for *Men's Journal*, Bourdain writes,

> "I have an operating principle that I am perfectly willing, if not
> eager, to believe that I'm completely wrong about everything. I have a
> tattoo on my arm, that says, in ancient Greek, 'I am certain of nothing.' I
> think that's a good operating principle. I love showing up to a place
> thinking it's going to be one way and having all sorts of stupid
> preconceptions or prejudices, and then in even a painful and embarrassing
> way, being proved wrong."

Bourdain was curious about what makes people happy and what their struggles
are, no matter where the person came from or what their place in society was.
That said, Bourdain notoriously came off as arrogant, and speaks of his own
vanity on several occasions. Especially later in Bourdain's life, he reflects on the
role that vanity has played in influencing his actions and feelings. In an
interview for *Men's Journal*, Bourdain writes,

> "If you're a writer, particularly if you're a writer or a storyteller of any
> kind, there is something already kind of monstrously wrong with you.
> Let's face it, it is an unreasonable attitude to look in the mirror in the
> morning and think, 'You know, there are people out there who would

really like to hear my story.' You know, 'I'm an interesting guy, and I have interesting things to say.' Look, the numbers overwhelmingly disprove that notion. It's an insane notion. Most writers fail. So the kind of drive — the kind of compulsion to spend a year or two of your life writing a book in the hope that people will buy it, that's what's called narcissism. An over-inflated sense of self."

What marked Bourdain's last days, however, perhaps more than all else was his love affair with the beautiful and accomplished actress and director, Asia Argento, and his powerful voice in the #MeToo movement and for feminism. It was while filming "Parts Unknown: Rome" that first brought the two together, and their easy camaraderie was an important feature of the episode. Asia Argento, Bourdain presents, is a single mother who lives in the outskirts of Rome with her two children. The two eat spaghetti while watching wrestling, join for a family meal with her children and sister, and discuss politics while walking around formidable, intimidating Roman architecture. Bourdain was in strong support of all of Argento's groundbreaking work for victims of sexual violence, stemming from her own rape by Harvey Weinstein, and began to put up photos celebrating Argento's beauty and soul on his social media platforms. Helen Rosner writes in her *New Yorker* article on Bourdain,

"Bourdain's sterling credentials as a man's man and a taker of no guff served as a bolster of the #MeToo movement at large. His unwavering support of Argento—as well as his ardent rejection of so much as a quantum of sympathy for famous chefs accused of transgression—brought him a new sort of celebrity as an activist … and uncompromising figure of moral authority." Argento notably gave a speech at Cannes where she spoke of her rape at the festival years earlier. "This festival was Harvey Weinstein's hunting ground," she spoke, voice full of emotion and power, and pointed out that many in the industry protected the culture of abuse that had prevailed for so long. "We are coming for you," she stated, her gaze reaching into all corners of the crowded auditorium. Bourdain was quick to bolster her reaction on social media, calling the speech an "unexpected nuke" on the crowd. In some ways, Argento's honest bravery did much to lay bare the sordid and monstrous reality of another shiny facade, not the gleaming restaurant but the gleaming screen. Bourdain and Argento shared over a year of what appeared to be a deep romantic and spiritual bond. According to Rose McGowan, a close friend and at times unofficial spokeswoman for Argento as well as a fellow Weinstein victim, the couple shared a 'free' relationship, and when people pointed the finger at Argento after pictures emerged of her with a French journalist, McGowan defended her friend in a letter in which she said attacking Argento would have been the last thing Bourdain wanted. Bourdain was clearly prompted into considering his own role in misogyny through his relationship with Argento. In an article for *Slate*, he apologized for what he saw as a failure to be an ally for women who were abused for years in the restaurant industry, and that he must have been projecting in some sense an ambivalent attitude towards women's rights through his immunity towards sexualized language in the kitchen and the all-boys culture that was in many kitchens. *Kitchen Confidential*, he remarked, was meant to be a type of cautionary tale against that misogynistic and testosterone-fueled culture, but he admitted that if he looked deeply into his work he might have seen subtle messages promoting antiquated and demeaning attitudes towards women. Notably, Bourdain had a hard time giving an answer to Rosner for *the New Yorker* as to whether he was a feminist when asked when at the beginning of his relationship with Argento. Rosner concludes the article with the anecdote that later on, after supporting Argento and seeing first-hand the trauma that sexual violence wreaks on women in the industry, Bourdain was with Rosner at a party and made sure to seek her out and let him know that if he couldn't answer before, to mark it down: "I'm a fucking feminist." Bourdain also celebrated on public media when Weinstein was indicted and posted the menu to the jail as a means of taunting the man. After Bourdain's death, Rose McGowan spoke up on accusations that Argento was to blame for his death. McGowan writes,

"When Anthony met Asia, it was instant chemistry. They laughed, they loved and he was her rock during the hardships of this last year. Anthony was open with his demons, he even wrote a book about them. In the beginning of their relationship, Anthony told a mutual friend, he's never met anyone who wanted to die more than him. Through a lot of this last year, Asia did want the pain to stop. But over their time together, thankfully, she did the work to get help, so she could stay alive and live another day for her and her children. Anthony's depression didn't let him, he put down his armor, and that was very much his choice. His decision, not hers. His depression won. Anthony and Asia had a free relationship, they loved without borders of traditional relationships, and they established the parameters of their relationship early on. Asia is a free bird, and so was Anthony. Was. Such a terrible word to write. I've heard from many that the past two years they were together were some of his happiest and that should give us all solace."

Throughout Bourdain's life, or second life, he cultivated friendships with several famous and important chefs. Most notably, Bourdain was extremely close personal friends with Eric Ripert, Fergus Henderson, Ferran Adrià, and Jose Andres. When Ferran Adrià closed El Bulli, it was Bourdain who was allowed in to film the preparation of every single dish on the menu, including meals that fed the waitstaff and kitchen staff. Eric Ripert appeared on multiple episodes of Bourdain's show and in the opening prologue to Bourdain's last memoir, *Medium Raw*. The scene opens in a chic bar of a restaurant in New York. Bourdain has received a mysterious invitation. At the bar he learns that some of the best chefs in the world have also received this invitation, and all sit, waiting and wondering. Bourdain quips that if something happened to that restaurant that evening, American fine dining would end right there. Eventually the men are lead into a giant dining room and they learn the motivation for the secrecy. On the menu are the infamous Ortolan birds, an endangered species which are no longer consumed in France but represent an important leg, or at least wrist, of French cuisine. The Ortolan birds were typically blinded and then gorged on millet and figs, drowned in Armagnac brandy and eaten whole, feet first. Bourdain contrasts this moment with a very different one; when he was in between drugs and jobs, flipping soggy English muffins and burgers at a lowly breakfast establishment in New York, a decade or more ago. Into this scene walks a girl who Bourdain admired at school for her creative spirit and "fabulousness," who is now a figure in the Downtown art scene. Bourdain cringes with embarrassment and describes his gratitude that she has the charity to pretend not to recognize him. Bourdain closes this dialogue with a question about whether he had it all wrong. "What could my memoir of an undistinguished—even disgraceful—career have said to people of such achievements?" he writes. "And who are these people anyway? Leaning back in their chairs, enjoying their after-dinner cigarettes, they look like princes. Are these the same losers, misfits, and outsiders I wrote about? Or did I get it all wrong?" Could the society of made chefs be as lonesome, dogged by doubt, and scarred as the cooks Bourdain knew as a junkie working at the lower register of Zagat? Do they recognize him, the cook who fucked up, as one of them? Bourdain may have been friends with some of the most important chefs in the world and eaten at the best restaurants, but he never, as it were, crossed over to the other side. You still had the impression after many years that Bourdain was a regular man in an exotic world, beaming back messages. John Birdsall wrote in a profile of Bourdain before his 60th birthday, "It makes me think of something *Lucky Peach* editor Peter Meehan told me about Bourdain, about how thinking of himself as an outsider fuels Bourdain. 'He feels fortunate to be there and tries to do the good work to keep his place at the table," Meehan said, "and that sets him apart. There is a moment in most people's careers that's like, 'I belong here.' I've never gotten that from Tony.'" Bourdain himself on his fame famously said, "I feel like I've stolen a car – a really nice car – and I keep looking in the rear-view mirror for flashing lights. But there's been nothing yet." Bourdain let his friendships enhance his life and his work without changing his self-image. These friendships opened doors, created new and fantastic experiences, and lasted until the very last years of his life.

Bourdain's suicide did not come from nowhere. Bourdain had written about suicidal urges on many past incidents, whether through the voices of his protagonists in his novels, who were repeatedly toying with the idea of driving off cliffs, or in light-handed comments made either on shows or in interviews. In a piece for *the New Yorker*, Rosner wrote, "In a 2016 episode of 'Parts Unknown,' set in Buenos Aires, he held an on-camera therapy session. 'I will find myself in an airport, for instance, and I'll order an airport hamburger,' he says, lying on a leather couch. 'It's an insignificant thing, it's a small thing, it's a hamburger, but it's not a good one. Suddenly, I look at the hamburger and I find myself in a spiral of depression that can last for days.'" Rosner was not the only one to pick up on Bourdain's potentially grave moods. Mario Bustillos, in a profile for *Eater magazine*, analyzed Bourdain's literary oeuvre and discovered that the writer had most likely based specific events in his novel off pieces of his own life. One recurring motif was the idea of driving his car off a cliff. This piece appeared in *Medium Raw* and consists of Bourdain himself discussing suicidal urges.

> "That's where I was in my life: driving drunk and way too fast, across a not very well lit Caribbean island. Every night. The roads were notoriously badly maintained, twisting and poorly graded. Other drivers... were, to put it charitably, as likely to be just as drunk as I was... I would follow the road until it began to twist alongside the cliffs' edges approaching the French side. Here, I'd really step on the gas... depending entirely on what song came on the radio next, I'd decide to either jerk the wheel at the appropriate moment, continuing, however recklessly, to careen homeward—or simply straighten the fucker out and shoot over the edge and into the sea."

Bustillos points out the similarities between this piece and Bourdain's fictional account in his novel.

"Leaving the Mariner's Club, he took the mountain route back to the pond, the scooter handling differently without Frances holding on in the rear... A few hundred yards ahead, the road took a steep drop down the other side of the mountain to the sea. The road was ungraded and unbanked; one could easily fly right off the side of that mountain, and Henry considered that option, toyed with the idea as if playing with himself, not serious, just to see how bad things were...

Bad manners to kill yourself. Realizing how drunk he really was, Henry started up the scooter and drove cautiously home."

The week before Bourdain hung himself in his hotel room, the prominent designer Kate Spade had also hung herself with a scarf in her room, and suicides can lead to other suicides as the event serves as a trigger. Bourdain's behavior was uncharacteristic for several days before the event. Bourdain was filming a show in the Alsace region of France, near Germany, to record a new episode for *Parts Unknown*. Bourdain failed to show up at breakfast at the luxury hotel, Le Chambard, in Kaysersberg village, the day before and, according to a friend he was with, had been in a dark mood. Bourdain was famously never late to anything, always arriving fifteen minutes before any appointment. When his time came to be on set, staff sent Eric Ripert, his best friend, to get Bourdain.

Ripert discovered Bourdain dead on June 8, 2018. Bourdain, who had been through intense ups and downs in his life through drug addiction and recovery and his late entry into the world of elite chefs and celebrity culture had this to say on handling pain. "I don't like it — it hurts, but if you cook food or write books or make television, it's like the tide — the weight will break on the beach. There is no stopping it. It will come, and then another wave, and then another wave. There's nothing you can do about it, and there's no point to railing against it. You've just got to toughen up. Learn to swim. I just suck it up." It could be presumed that Bourdain's defenses finally gave in, and 'sucking it up' was not enough. The depression that had chased Bourdain throughout his life finally overtook him.

The grief of the loss of Bourdain was felt around the world. The next day, fans papered the windows of Les Halles, the last restaurant where Bourdain worked, with loving notes and remembrances. Some fans reacted with anger, like Val Kilmer, who wrote this message after his death, "Oh the dark thick pain of loss. The selfishness," Kilmer said. "How many moments away were you from feeling the love that was universal. From every corner of the world you were loved. So selfish. You've given us cause to be so angry." Most fans reacted with the reflection that Bourdain had been a true friend, a humanitarian, and had opened their worlds through their TV screens. Those that met Bourdain called him full of life and energy. Argento asked that people give her privacy, calling Bourdain her "love, protector and rock." Eric Ripert spoke of his best friend, "praying that he is at peace." President Obama focused on the legacy of Bourdain's work, saying "he taught us about food, but more importantly about its power to bring us together." Bourdain's mother was caught off-guard, saying she had no idea anything was wrong and that she was full of surprise, saying that "he was the last person in the world who would have done something like this." For many, Bourdain represented someone who had accomplished his goals and who had access to the best parts of life and culture. Bourdain was tall, handsome, wealthy and interesting. For Bourdain to take his own life seemed to shock people and their assumptions about happiness and human psychology. A deeper look at Bourdain's life, however, shows a man of great feeling and nuance, one who fought great internal battles for much of his life. After the tragedies of Spade and Bourdain, an important national dialogue was triggered about depression.

Bourdain left an indelible impact upon the world, and in the days since his death his book sales skyrocketed. Bourdain had travelled to nearly a hundred countries when he died and had filmed almost two hundred and fifty television episodes, revisiting several countries many times. Bourdain himself became a

cultural icon, appearing as himself in movies like *The Big Short*. Bourdain won

four Emmy Awards and was nominated for 23 more. Much of Bourdain's work,

however, could be the establishment in our consciousness of a questioning

archetype, a gadfly, and let us know that just like in the restaurant establishment,

there is often much more than what we are shown, hiding just beneath the

surface. Bourdain taught us to value our fellow man, value ourselves, and eat

well.

.

Printed in Great Britain
by Amazon

67197755R00025